THE COLORING BOOK FOR KIDS AND ADULTS

I0464998

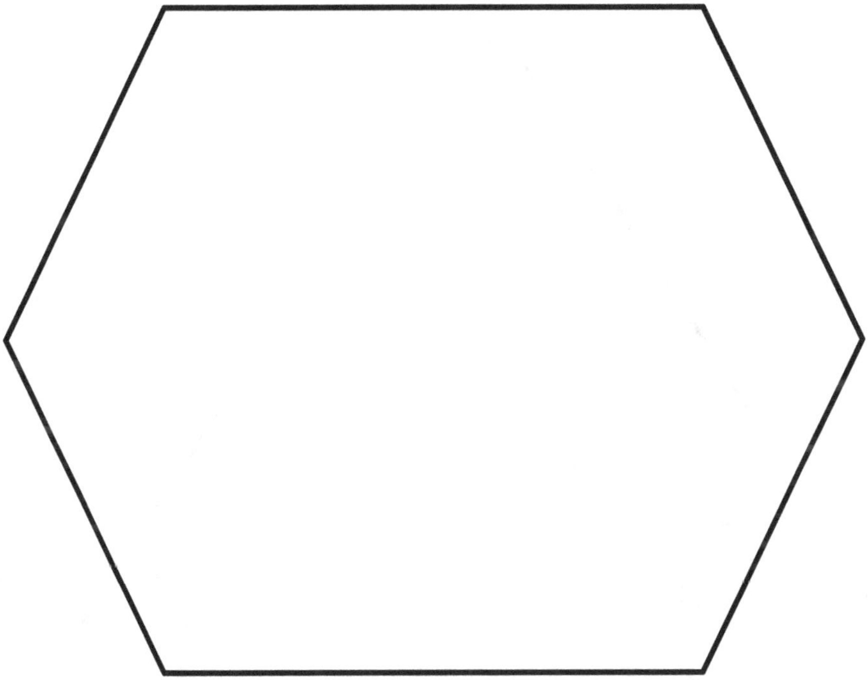

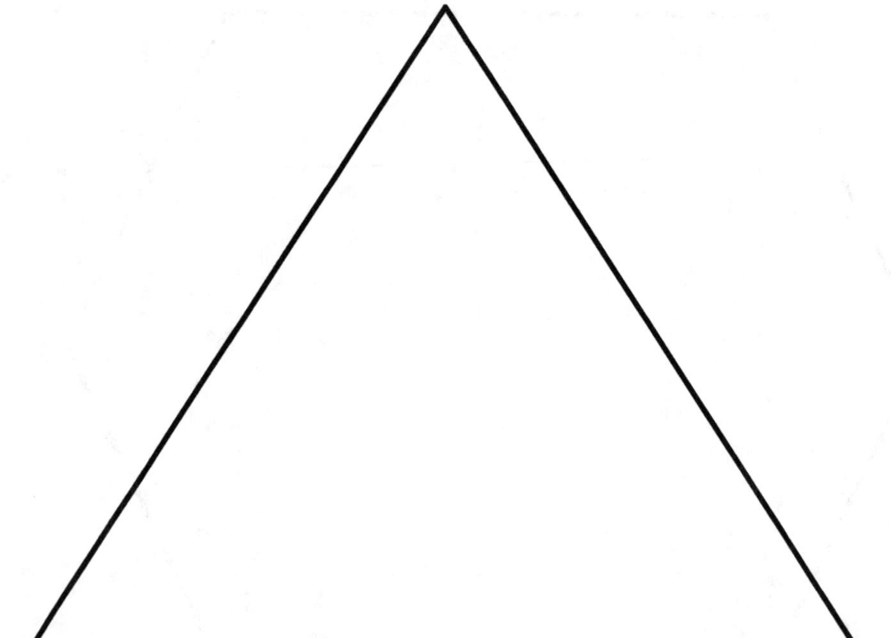

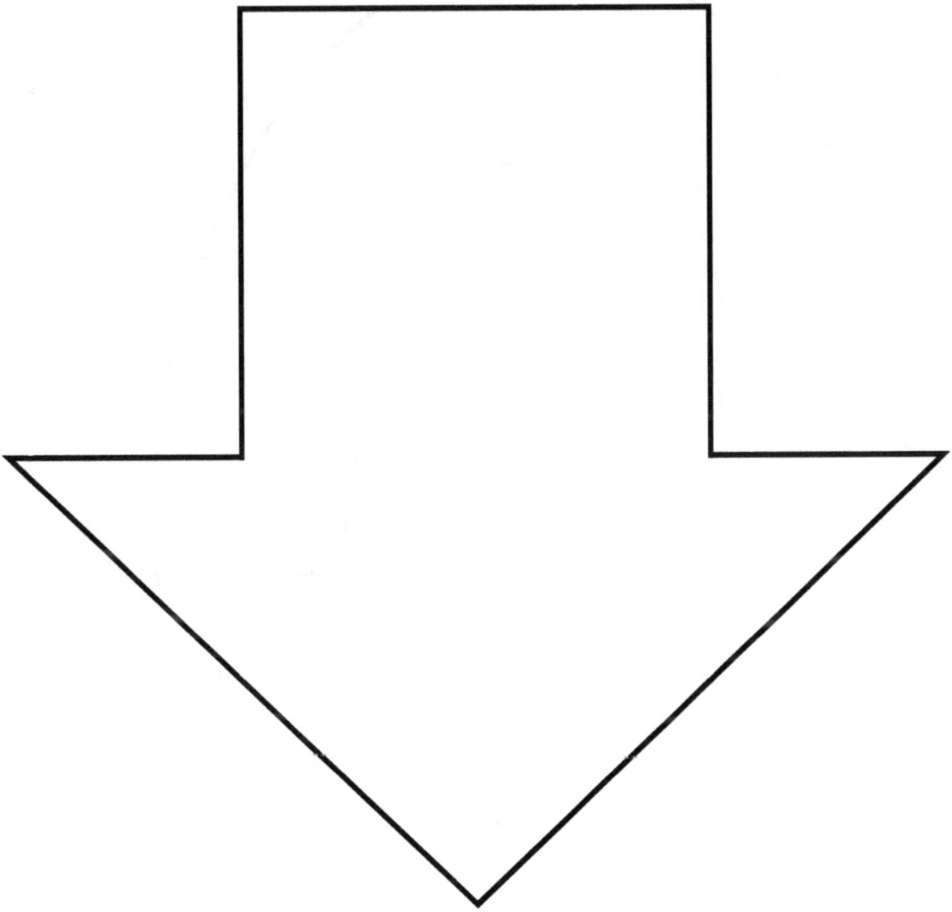

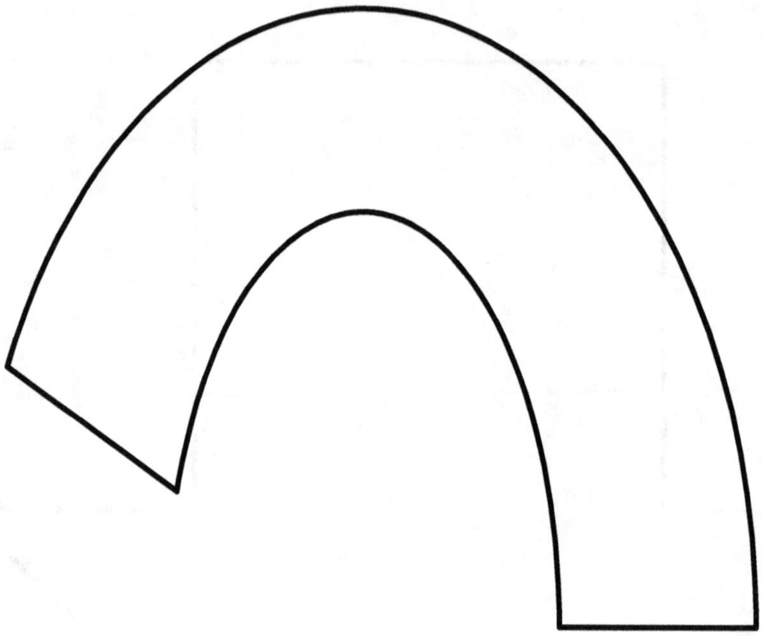

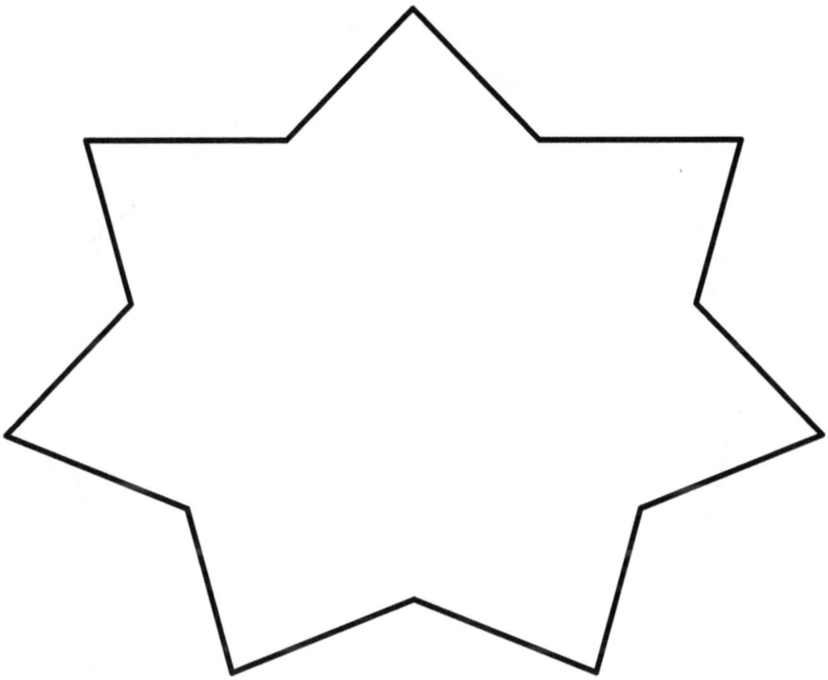

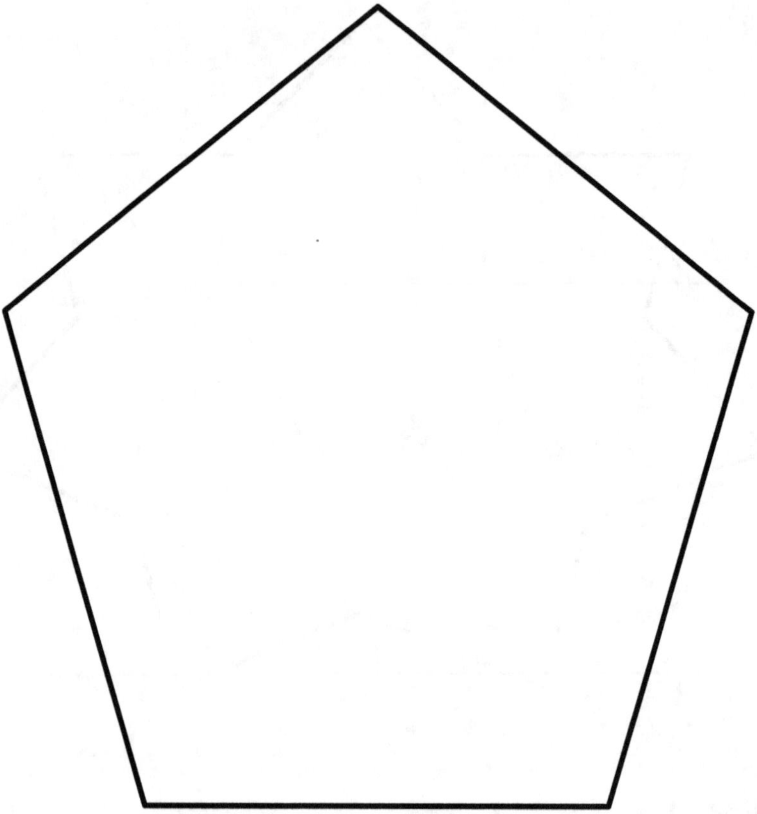

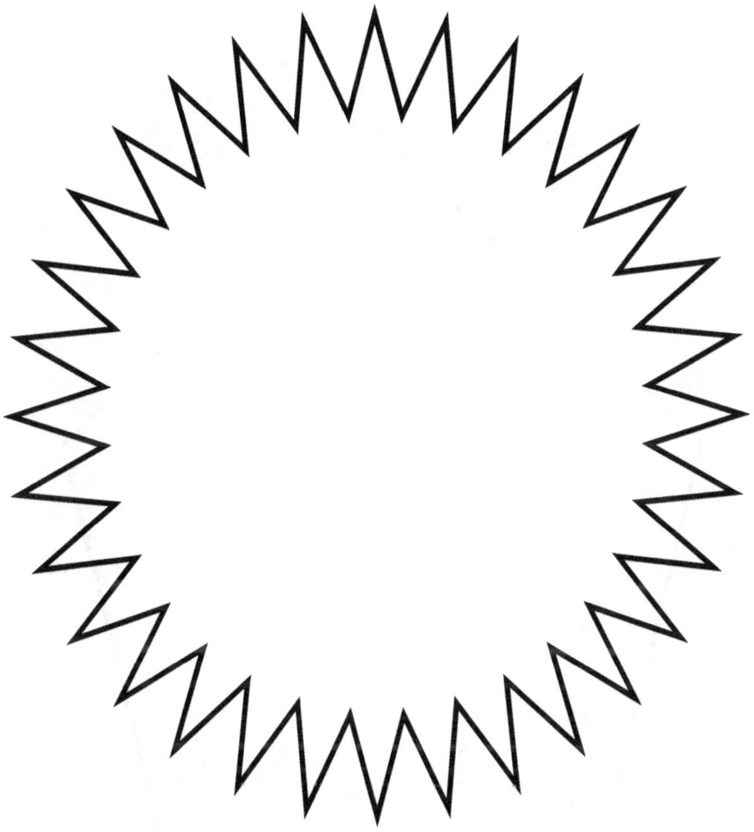

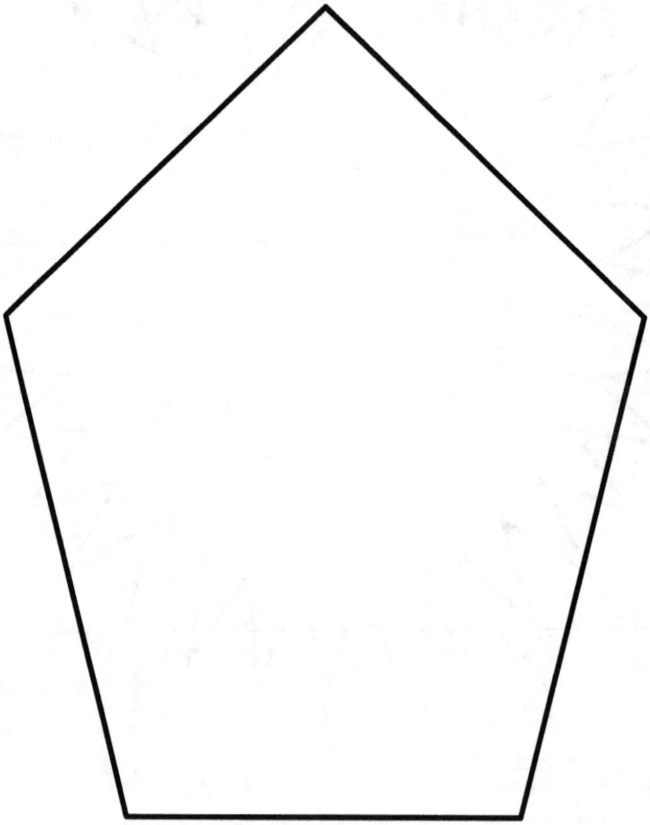

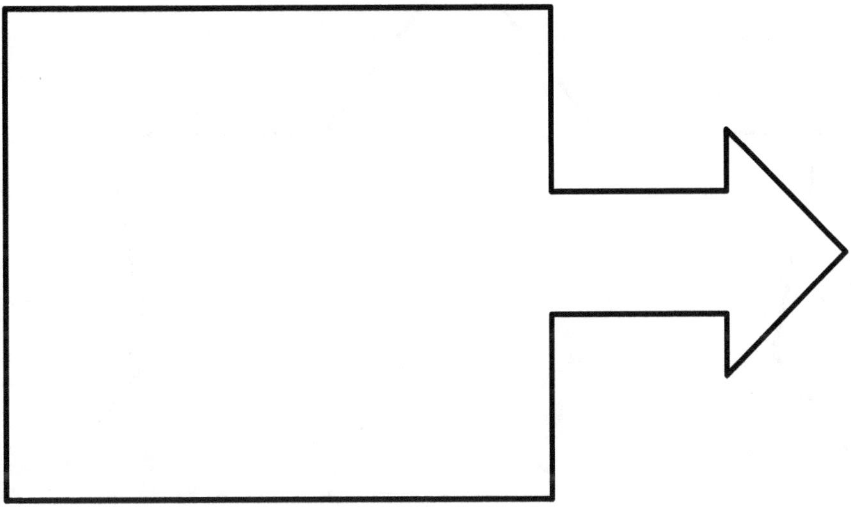

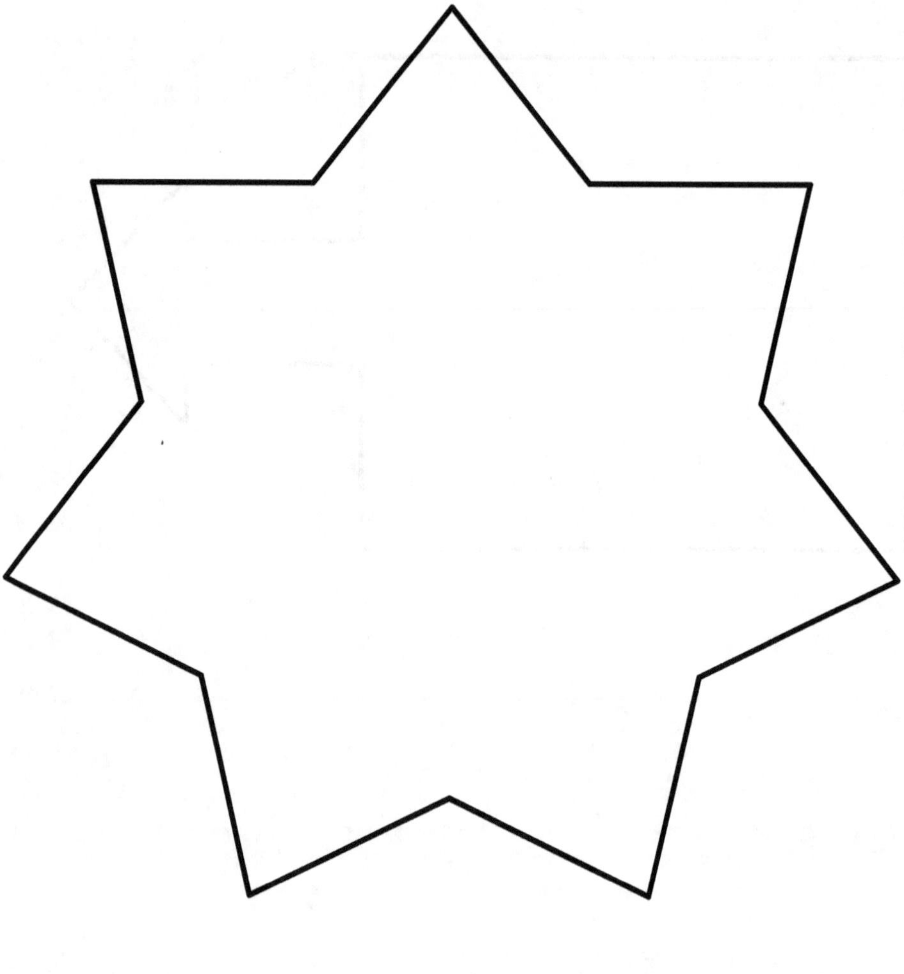

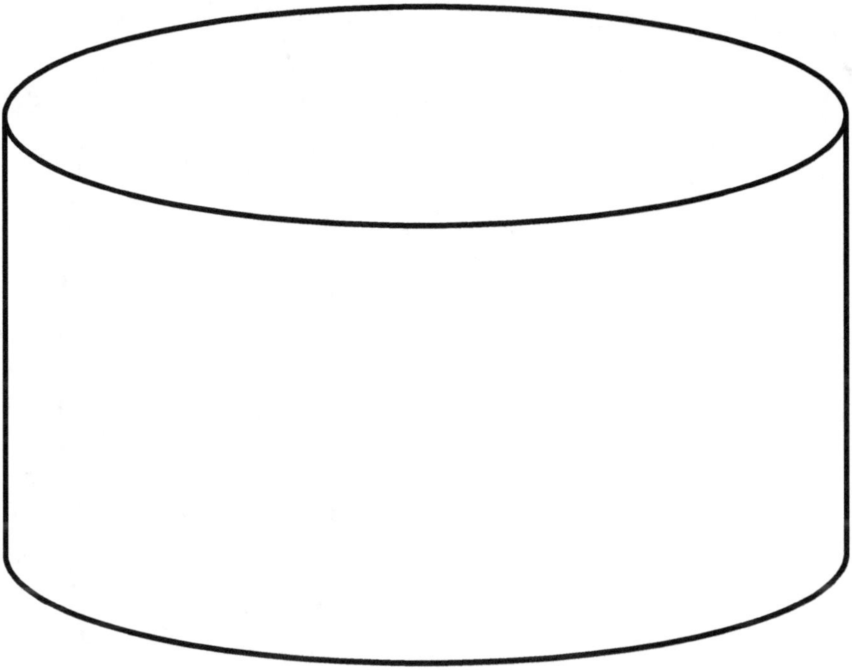

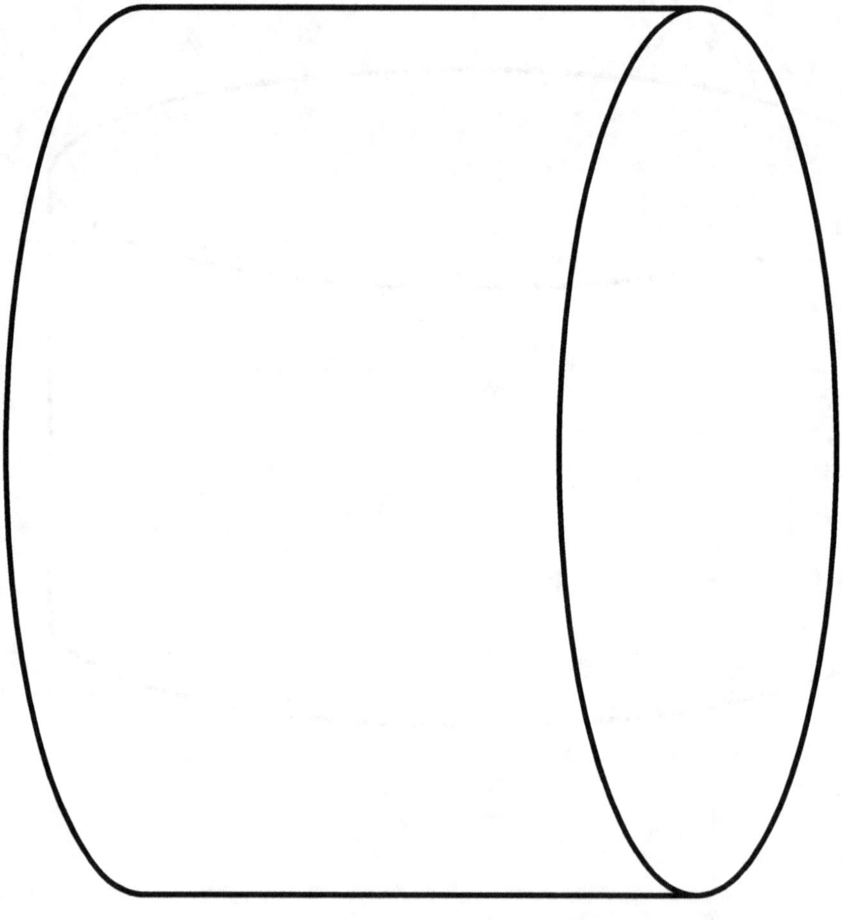

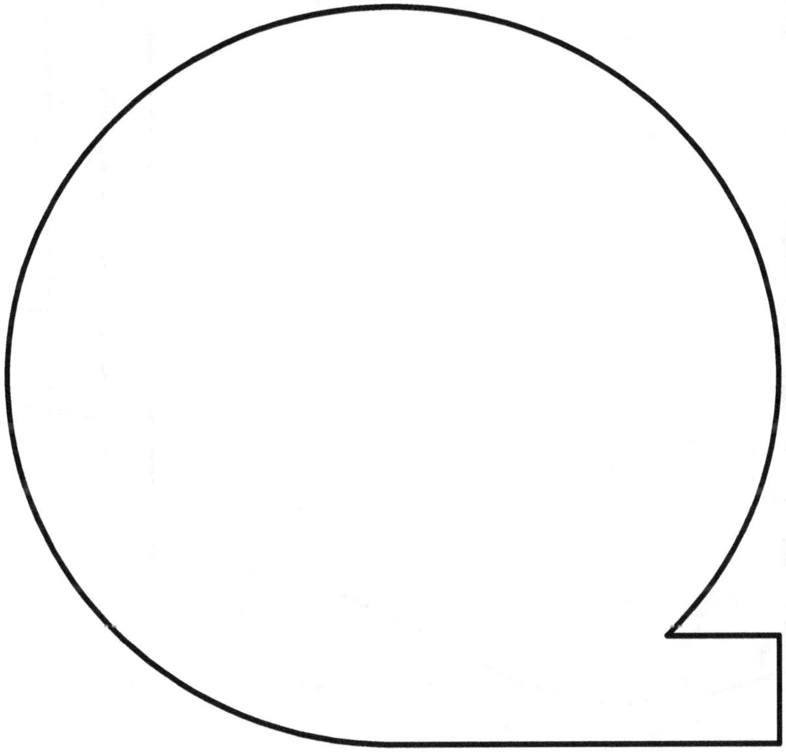

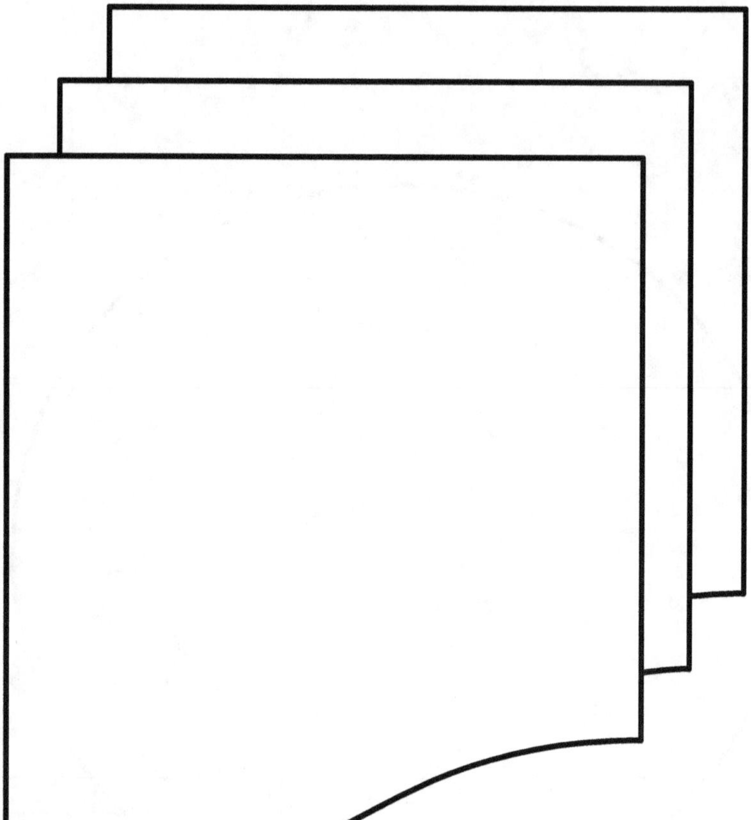

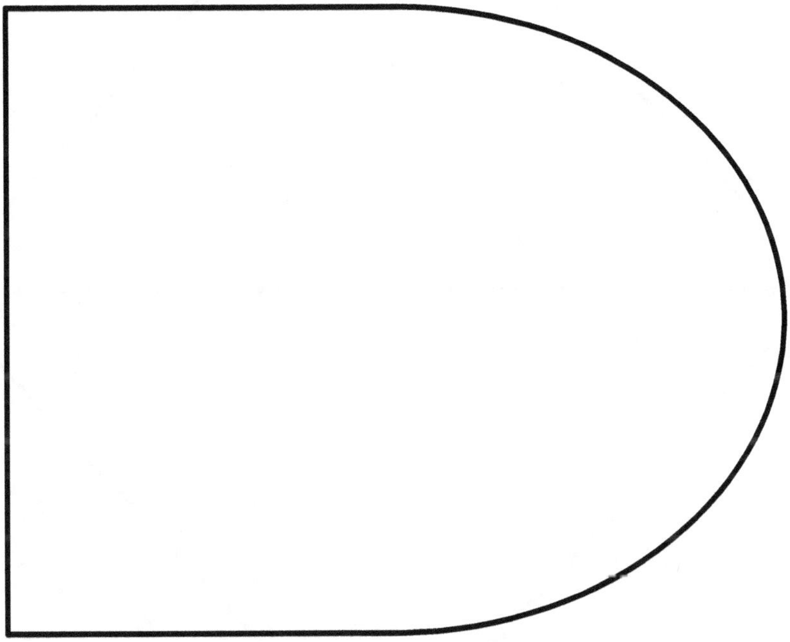

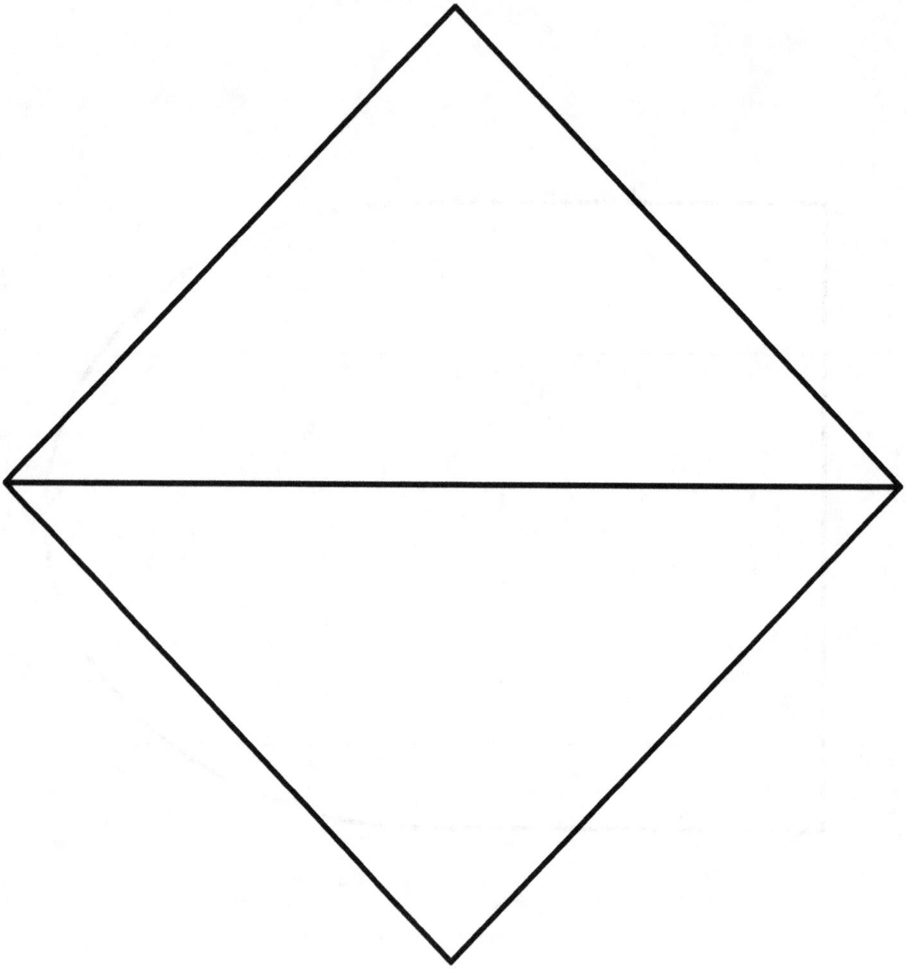

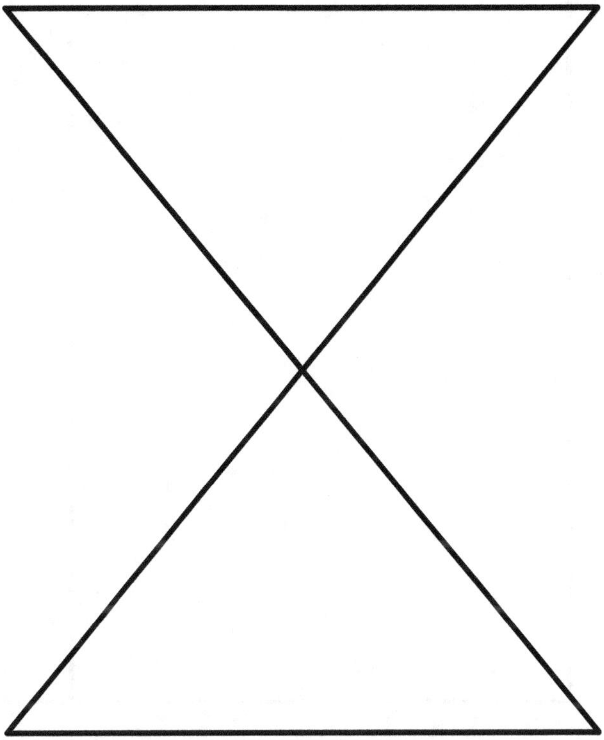

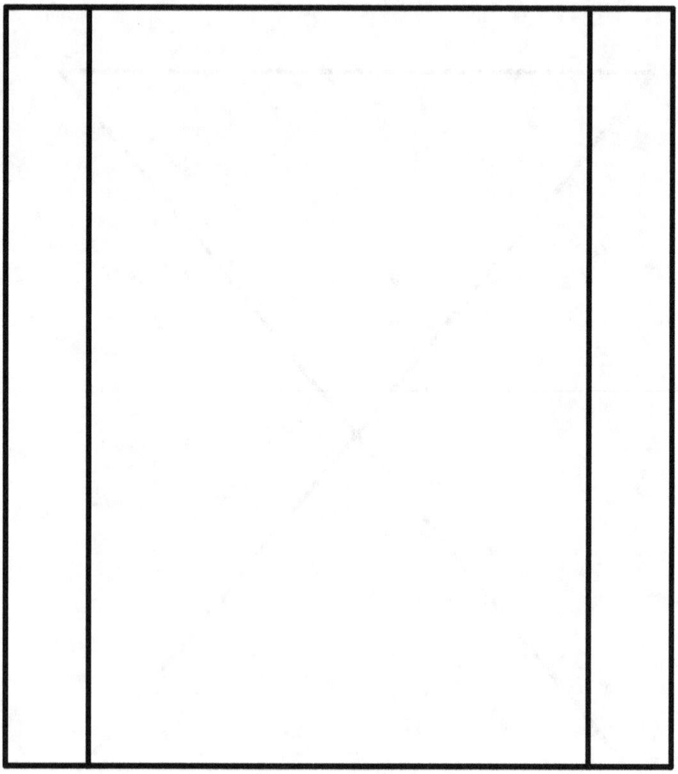

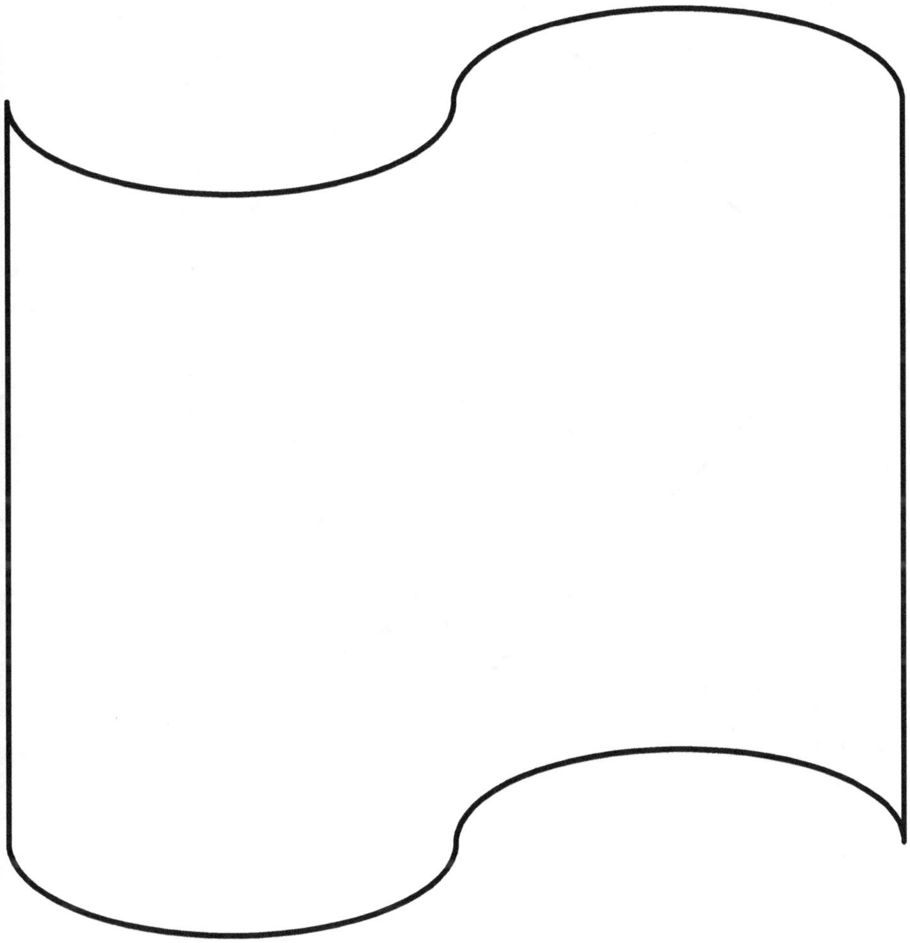

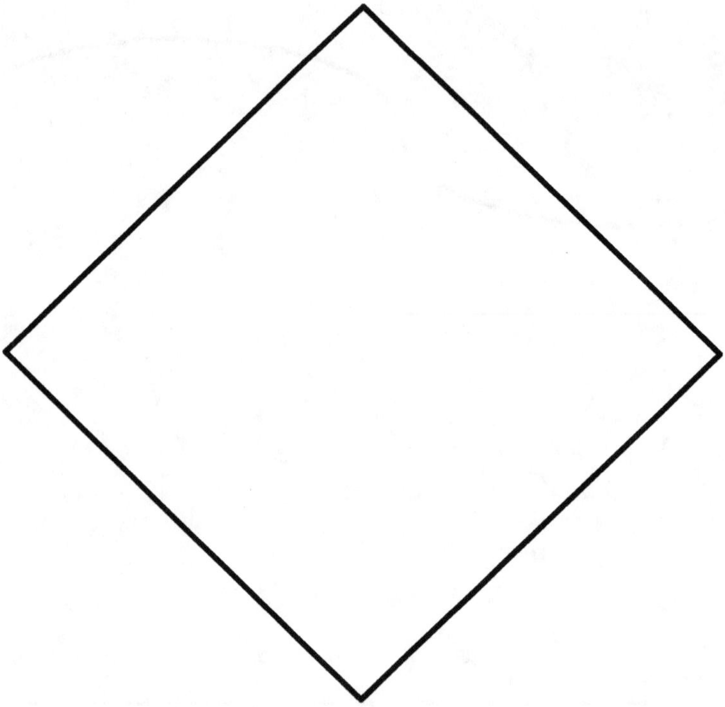

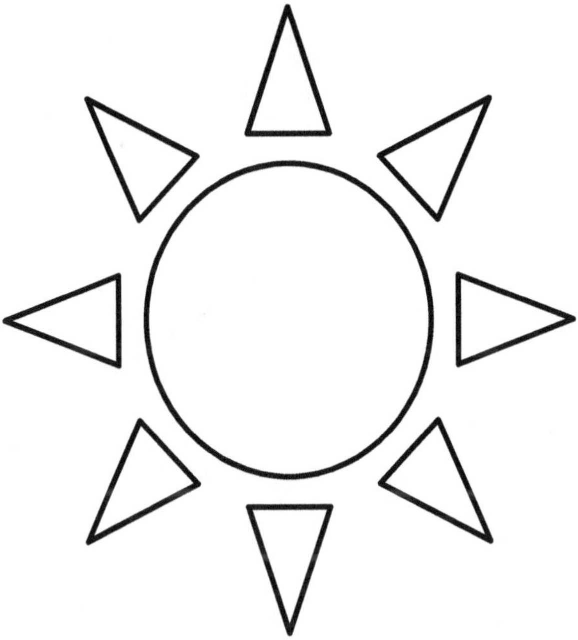

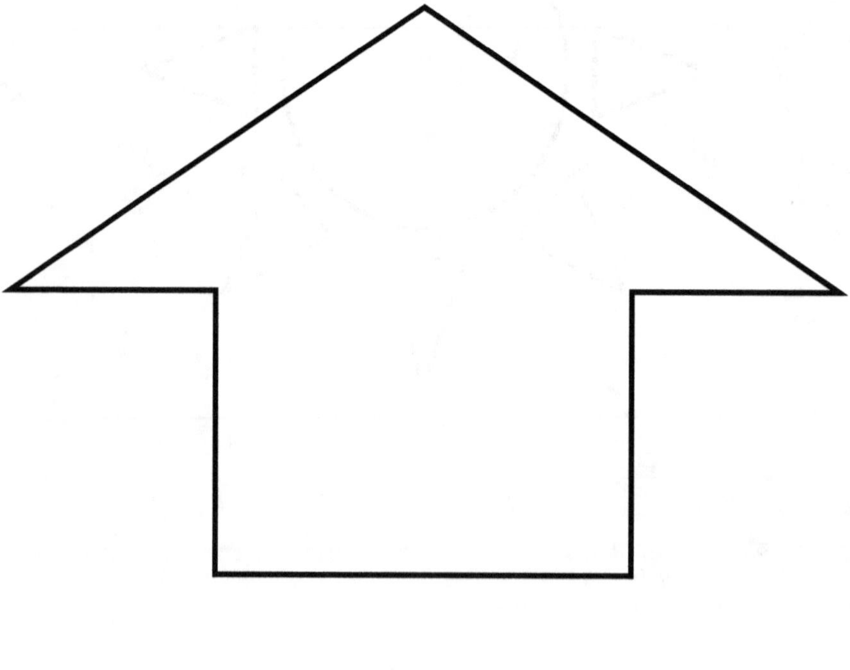

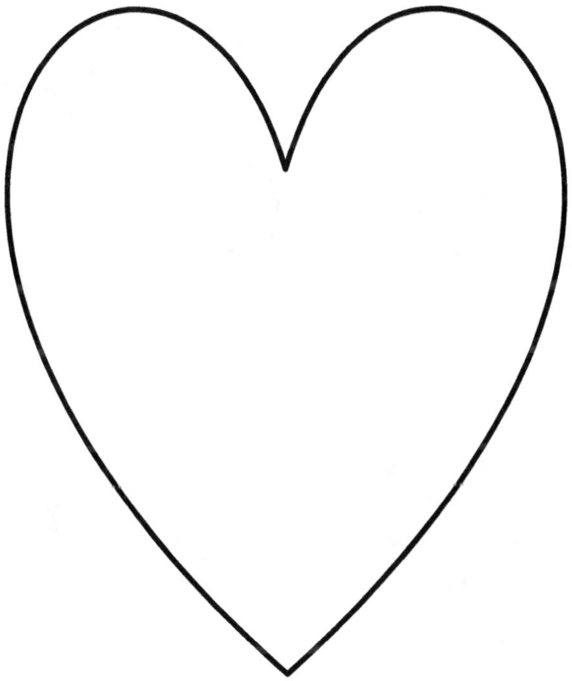

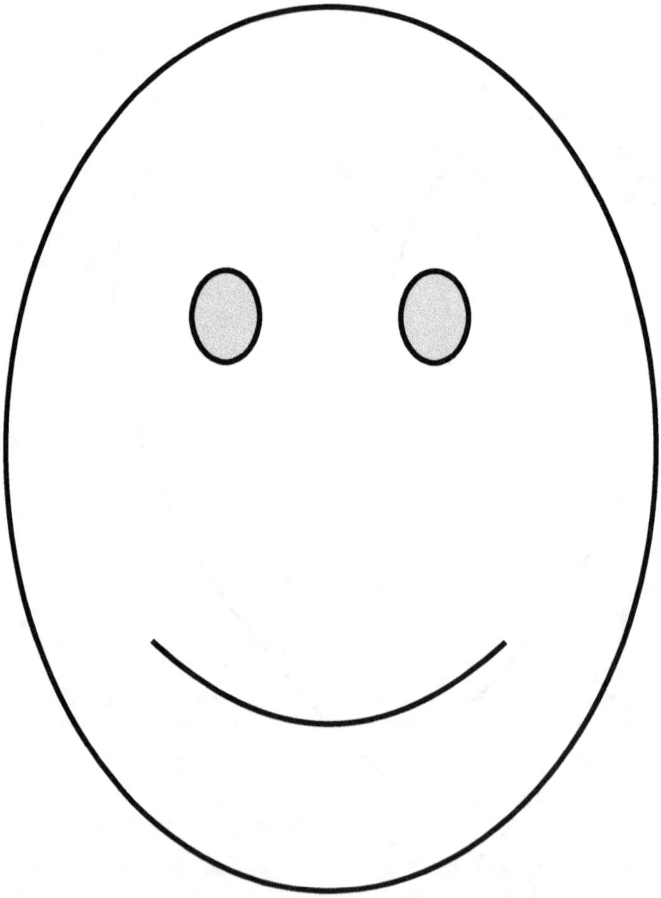

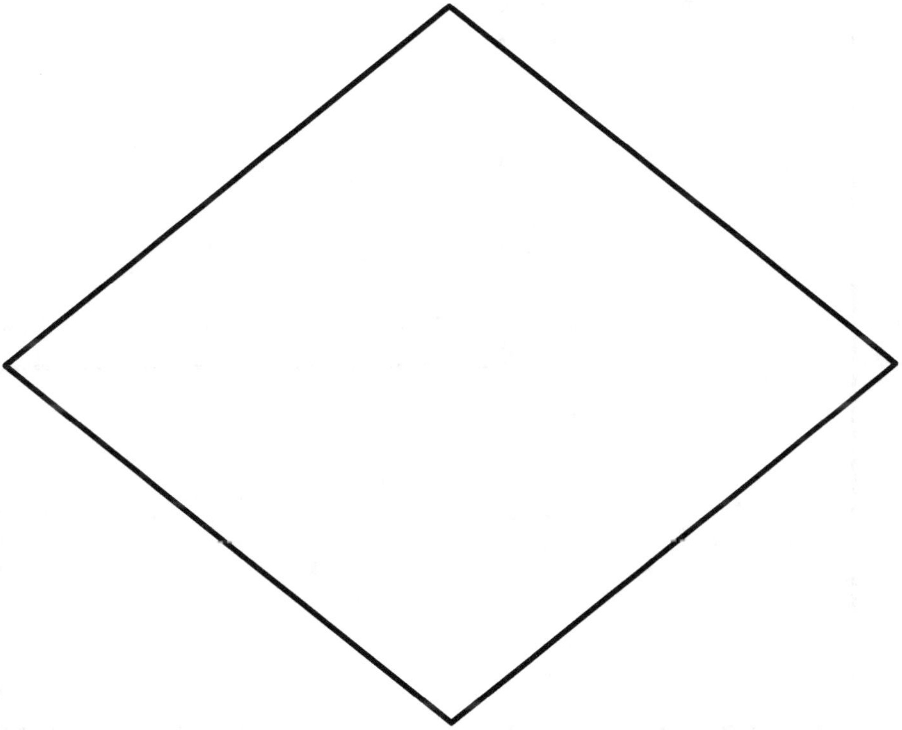

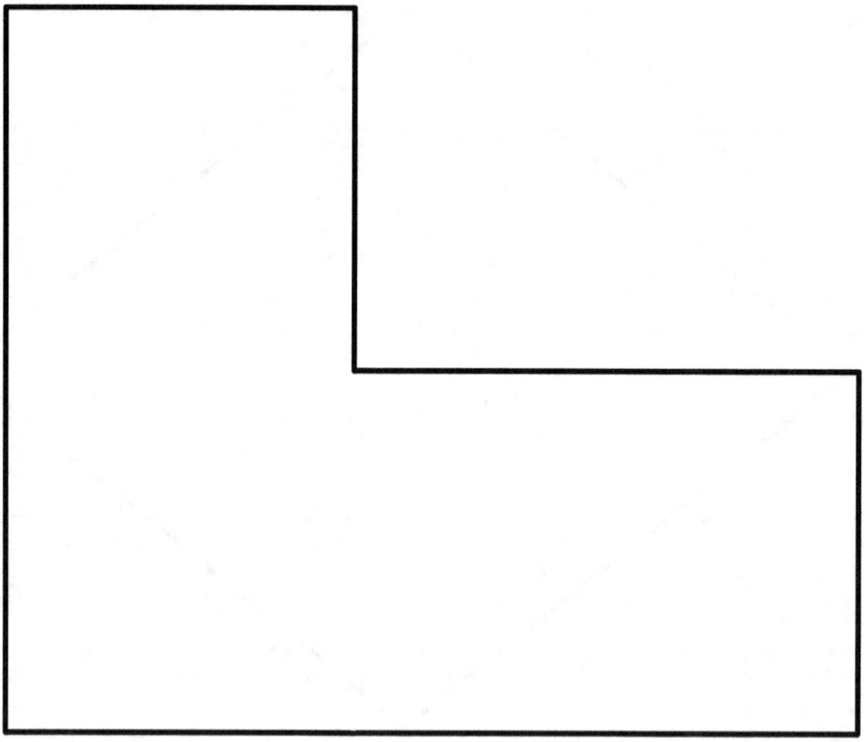

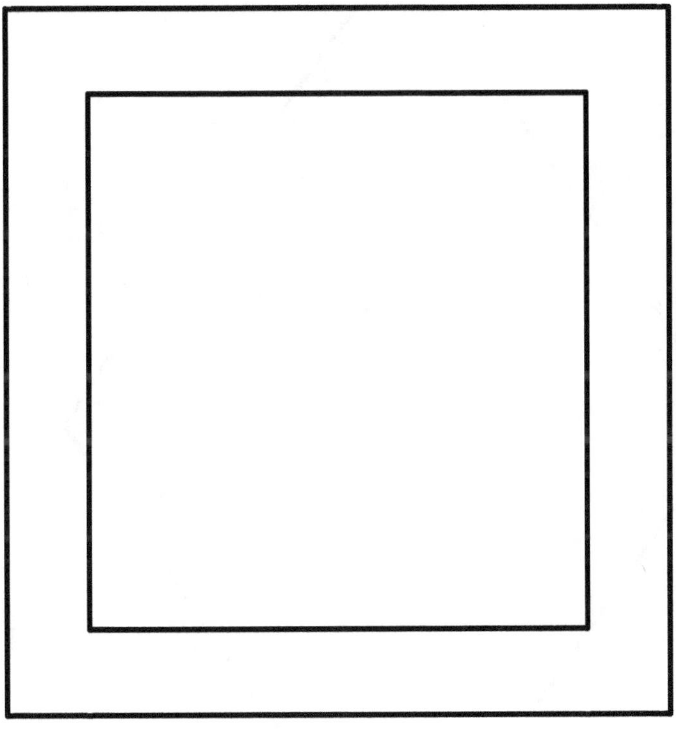

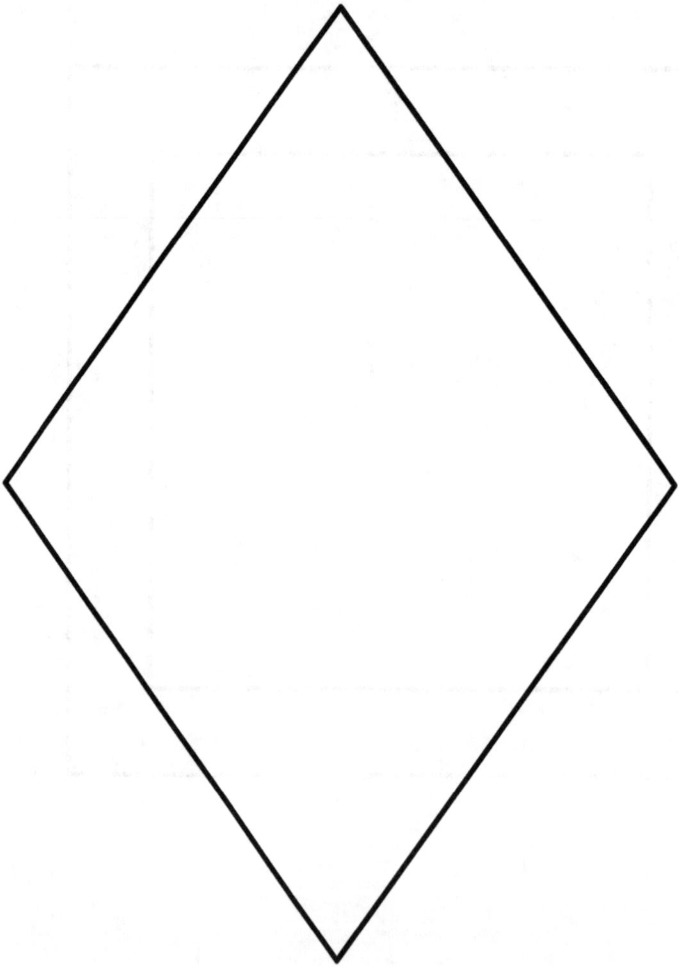

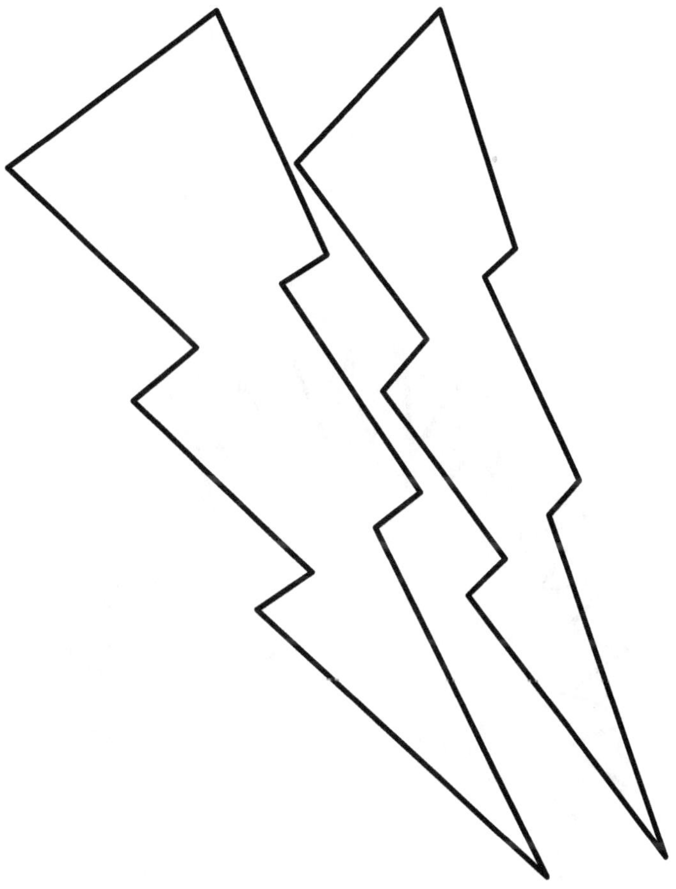

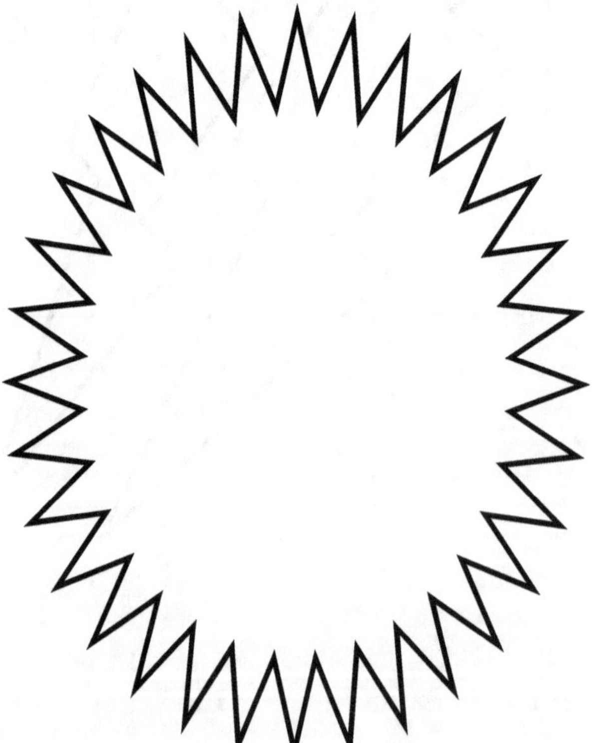

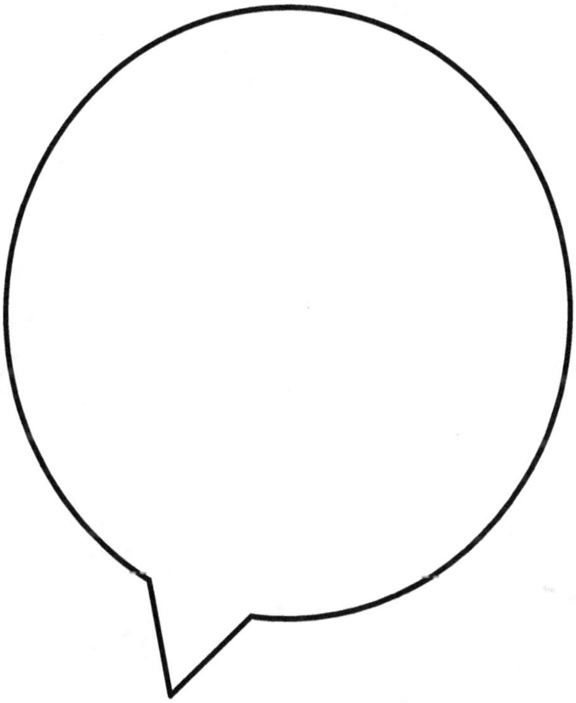

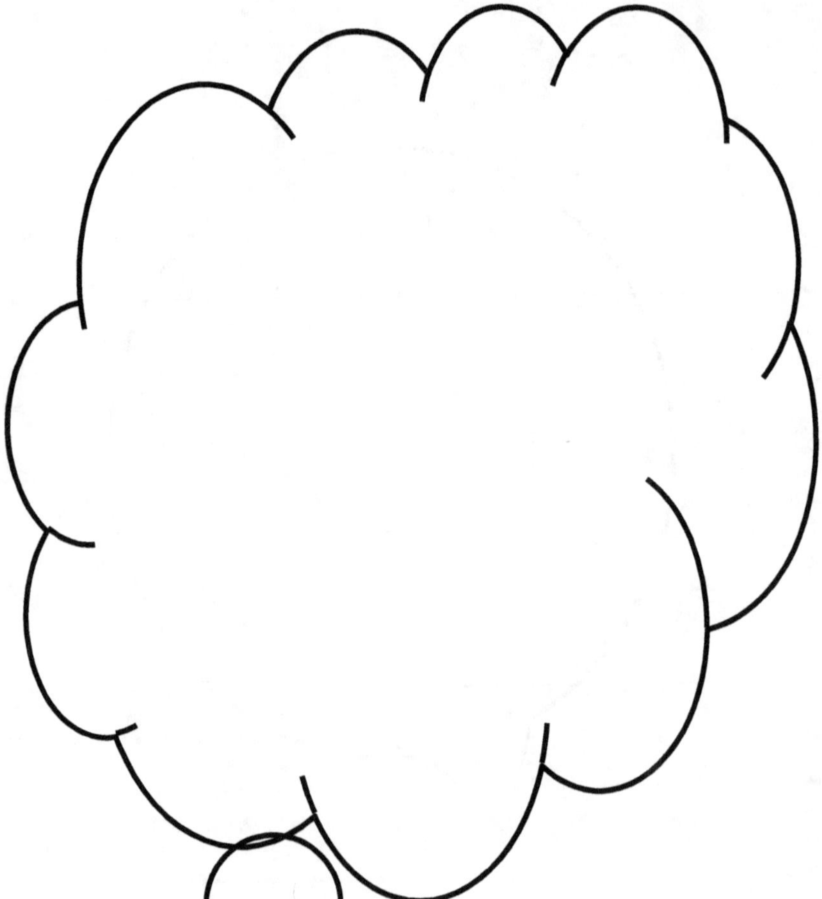

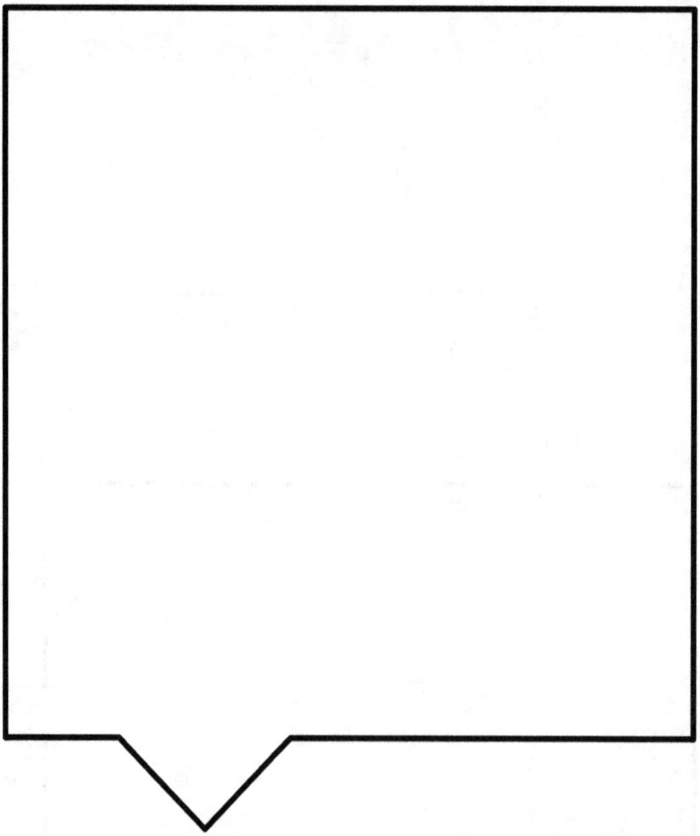

www.ingramcontent.com/pod-product-compliance
Lightning Source LLC
Chambersburg PA
CBHW070752180526
45168CB00004B/1590
9781511826471